To be alive is power,

Existing in itself,

Without a further function,

Omnipotence enough.

—Emily Dickinson

The tumult and the shouting dies,

The Captains and Kings depart.

Still stands Thine ancient sacrifice---

A humble and a contrite Heart.

Lord God of Hosts, be with us yet,

Lest we forget, lest we forget.

—Rudyard Kipling.

This book will raise more questions than answer,

hopefully you will revisit some of your perspectives.

Graceful Exits.

Other titles this book could have had?

1. Learn Lessons move on, drop baggage.
2. Power vs. Force.
3. The Power of Intimacy.
4. Mistake's were made. (But not by me.)
5. What About Bob. Am I going to die?
6. Because I'm Good Enough, Smart Enough and Doggone it people like me.
7. Arguing with the Mirror.
8. All bleeding stops.
9. If not good enough without a Gold Medal, won't good enough with.
10. Are the NCAA and NFL-level playing fields? Show business, not friendship?
11. Always drink upstream from the head.
12. There will be bad time's, but they will always remind you of the good times you weren't paying attention too.

Irish Poem, "I wish you Enough."

I wish you enough sun to keep your attitude bright no matter how gray the day.

I wish your enough rain to appreciate the sun and the gray days.

I wish you enough happiness to keep your spirit alive and everlasting.

I wish you enough pain so that even the smallest of joy is valued.

I wish you enough gains to satisfy your wanting's.

I wish you enough loss to appreciate all you possess.

I wish you enough hellos to get you through the good-byes.

This book is extending feelings to all the people I love and who are reading it. Feelings I have extended to loved ones and want to say again or never have extended.

I'm not beholden to force the opposite of power. Are you?

Good to no longer be smartest or dumbest or any other Est.

I like Noblesse oblige.

I write this book with a tear and a smile. I believe the opposite of depression is expression even if your a introvert like Lincoln.

When I have power struggles with others, that really displaced anger at myself. It's powerful to process displaced anger for me and not go through life with a ball and chain.

Magic in dialogues for me with Life, you, then me.

A miracle is a change of perspective not necessarily positive, I like darkness to light not fake positive thinking. How about you?

Eleanor Roosevelt said, no one can make you feel inferior without your consent, that includes myself.

"If policeman follows you for 500 miles, you're going to get a ticket." Warren Buffett.

Contents:

Introduction..1

Preface..5

Chapter 1: Wall St. Fed Reserve, Banksters..............21

Chapter 2: Is the Civilization Process Working?.........33

Chapter 3: Bottom Feeders?..............................45

Chapter 4: Who's On First?..............................49

Chapter 5: J F K ?......................................53

Chapter 6: Drunk on Power or Force?.....................59

Chapter 7: Mendacity & Sulphur..........................63

Chapter 8: Addiction: Pitiful attempt self-medication?..67

Conclusions...71

Conclusions, Part II....................................81

Bibliography..91

The Person in the Arena, by Teddy Roosevelt.

It's not the critic who counts; not the person who points out how the strong person stumbles, or where the doer of deeds could have done better.
The credit belongs to the person who is in the arena, whose face is marred by dust and blood; who strives valiantly; who errors; who comes up short again and again, because there is not effort without error and shortcomings; but who actually strives to do the deeds; who knows the enthusiasms and devotions.
Who spends themselves in a worthy cause who at best knows in the end the triumph of high achievement, and who at worst, if fails, at least fails whole daring, so that their place will never be with souls who know neither victory or defeat.

PS I believe it's wise not to be in the arena all the time. Teddy died young.

Graceful Exits.

There's a trick to a graceful exit. It begins with the vision to accept when a job, relationship, life stage is over---and let go. It means leaving what's over without denying it's validity or past important in our life.
A belief every exit line is a entry, that we are moving on not out. The trick of retired may be the trick of living well. It's hard to recognize that life is not a holding action, but a process and we don't leave our best parts behind. We own what we experienced back there, these times are part of life now and when we exit, we take ourselves along---quite gracefully. Ellen Goodman.

Introduction

I'm an American Capitalist, believe in the Better Angels of Our Nature and Tender Mercies. Powers that Be is a hardball topic. Your interpretation is as valid as mine.

This book is obviously subjective. It briefly goes back to 50,000 BC, when women were God's and men slugs and gofers. (still are just don't know it.) We conned women into believing there was a Devil and we would protect them.

This work is not about history, it's about power and perspective and interpretations Okay?

I like the idea that opinions don't have to be facts, just simply how you or I feel. Yet, I'm sure you don't have to take my opinions or facts seriously. I like feelings are never wrong, but often inaccurate. I believe feeling are over-rated and under-rated.

I have more power struggles being right than wrong. In a zero sum game someone has to be wrong for me to be right.

I love Felix Frankfurter's quote "There are issues about

which people of reasonable good will disagree." Question is what is reasonable goodwill?
Most women's DNA is more domestic than a male's and that's changing. Most women wouldn't send their son or daughter to a dumb political war, like Vietnam or Iraq. No disrespect to our Military. (your opinion please?)

Then I jump from 50,000 BC, to Julius Caesar, Lincoln, Teddy Roosevelt and the Man in the Arena. Eleanor and FDR (note I mention Eleanor first), then Harry Truman, then JFK and the best and brightest, lastly current demonstrations of Power. This work in not really not about politics or history, but Power.

Maybe power is about What or Who has your back?

Maybe power isn't about luck. Luck to me is work---and realizing what is and isn't a opportunity.

Graceful exits are powerful for me, but Graceful is not always easy.

Power seems to change daily, meaning what I may have some influence over or related too. Power is really about who's in charge of the butter, like the story of Bill Bradley's roost.

It's interesting to watch people in power over-play their hand and get shut down. I think Hillary Clinton lost the election referring to the opposition as "a bundle of deplorable's." That may have energized some voters on the fence. I have interviewed many asking, do you think about power much? Do you have any experience with Power? How do you define?

I let some read this manuscript and got some good feedback as usual. Some didn't like my humor and found it offensive. So I revisited and made some adjustments.

This book isn't about humor, so no excuses if you don't like my attempts.

I like quotes like "It not that I loved Caesar less, it's that Love Rome." Of course Caesar's remark via Shakespeare "Cassius has a lean and hungry look, is dangerous dissatisfied and hungry for Power" is fascinating.

I'm not a Christian, yet Jesus made a super powerful statement to Pilot, he said "you have no power over me unless my Father gives it to you."

I hope you will give my some feedback from your view, will ask often "What say you?"

How you interpret this work depends on your mood or feelings. I like to acknowledge feelings yet not take as guides. I think my feelings are often over-rated and under-rated.

The point is power is real, yet today I can be a dust mop, tomorrow a peacock. I've been a Mortgage Banker or Bankster as some say most of my life. Was also President and

Chairman of Board of a Corporation. Power is fleeting.

I believe there is power in kindness yet forget to be kind and put myself in timeout to regain my humanness. Deep distresses has humanized my soul just like most of civilization.

I believe that mistakes are part of being human and learning from makes me human. As C.S. Lewis said "What you too? I thought I was the only one."

I didn't vote for President Trump, but it was fascinating to see him beat the Democrats, Republican establishment, Wall St. and Media. That's power.

I love dialogues vs. monologues so please respond if you wish. I'm sure this probably isn't your first rodeo or mine.

Caution: if you offend me you may wake up with a dead horses head in your bed.

Do you know Christ was only on the cross three hours?

Somehow when I seem superior I'm always a victim too?

I used to be different, now I'm the same.

Yet, dust to dust was not spoken of our Soul.

Michael

Preface

I have believed for years that one of the worst vices is advice. Like I have to love me before I can love you. I'm not held back by the love I did or didn't get in a secure base. I'm held back by the love I'm not giving.

Be yourself is another I'm skeptical of. Means I'm not being myself and separated and not okay. This too will pass another bit of bad advice for me. This is passing now. Will pass separates. I'm as connected as Nuclear fusion, made of the same stuff as our stars. If I want to be cut off and uniquely better or worse and suffer that's by freedom. I like inclusiveness.

My sister and brother are as right as me. Yet there are healthy boundaries. Trees do not grow to the sky.

If you're not at the table, you're on the menu. Not really, just another fear based bit of Fake News in my opinion. Power is knowing which options I have and the ability to access.

What do you call a Lawyer with an IQ of 60? Your honor. This book will be irreverent. I claim no moral high ground.

I like "Lord help me forgive those who make different mistakes or errors that I do."

I paid to have this book edited and there are mistakes in the transmission, some correct words were changed to incorrect. That's reality, no excuses. This book is not about the Kings English and I'm an amateur writer, like Bobby Jones was an amateur golfer.

David Hawkins in his classic book Power vs. Force shows a map of consciousness from 0 to 1000. Anything below 200 is Force, above Power. Maybe sometimes both can be happening? Depends on the individual and how define Power.

One I like is: Power is the ability to change or prevent change. Many like to keep people subordinate and some like it, like the people that followed Jones and committed suicide. Yes power in the wrong hands is lethal.

Two young fish going downstream. Older fish going other way said "Hi, how is the water? Neither said anything kept swimming, then one said to other, "What the Hell is Water?

So this book asks each of you, what is Power, how have you experienced Power or maybe how can I be disempowered?

Sometimes to me what seems like power is force. Force = Counterforce and sometimes the counterforce is the power.

I find there are different kinds of power. Lower like physical hitting or screaming. In Sparta when an important issue was debated, whoever yelled the loudest won the contest. That's force not power.

I won't be yelling in this offering. In fact will come close to whispering. I cherish this opportunity beyond the measure of words.

Higher Power is like "Mercy is mightiest in the mightiest." That's unconditional love even though I may not agree, I know you have your music and drummer. You're as right as I am. Can being right be a form of violence?

I like talking like I'm right and listening like I'm wrong. That gives you the right to feel as you do right now and me too. I like resigning from the debating society with myself, others and life. I used to be different, now I'm the same, meaning more alike than not.

No apologies for preface or repetitions or errors, nobody is perfect in my reality. Repetition pierces even the dullest of minds and has awakened me to reality. I love Groucho Marx, he said I'm not crazy about reality, but it's the only place to get a good meal.

As a journalist I don't believe in burying the Leads. Here we go Okay?

A Prudent Powerful person is one who thinks it is more important what Fate has conceded, than what it has denied. Balstar Grecian.

This book isn't going to try to change you. I can't change me, so I'm not a threat to your cup of tea or music. Agreed, okay?

I have learned there are people who love me dearly, that just don't know how to express their feelings. (been there.)

Enough is never enough for the person whom enough is to little. Ancient Greek quote.

Hope to get you to participate in this book like it's a conversation or dialogue with you and me, rather than a monologue one way street. I will ask, What say You? Please let me know the Best and Worst Advice you ever got and I will put it in the next edition?

Hope you will respond Pro or Con at Maudley3@aol.com, after your read.

One of my all-time quotes and it's not holier than thou, is: "I never met a person in whom I failed to recognize some superior quality to myself; If they were older, I said they had done more good than me; if they were younger, I said they had make fewer mistakes; if richer I said they had given more to charity; if poorer, I said they had suffered more; if wiser, I know nobody is perfect. Take this to heart my friend." (Jewish Prayer.)

I feel like it's worth every treasure on earth to be young at Heart. Picasso said, it takes a long time to become Young at Heart.

McGeorge Bundy said "Gray is the color of truth." Not for me. Truth is colorful for me, not always gray or black and white. Power is the same for me.

Power for me is being Stoic sometimes doing what's right no matter how I feel.

Very often Power for me is not asking a cruel question. Some questions are best not asked. Many have let me save face by being kind. Honesty is not always the best policy. Honesty without kindness is cruelty. That's Force not Power in my experience.

I'm a big Sinatra fan. In his book, The Way You Wear Your Hat, in late life he said, my ambition is to pass on to others interested, what I know. It has taken me a long, long time to learn what I know now, and I don't want that to die with me. He said only a fool is careless and doesn't know the odds before they act. And it's good to scratch each other's back, you can't always reach the itch yourself. Heartfelt appreciation, Francis Albert.

I used to audition presenters in the seminar business. I liked to remind them this isn't life and death that Life is not an audition for after life either. Okay if it is for you but not me. I like being born every day and saying check please every night. Fresh starts and Graceful exits.

Guy walked into meeting, everyone noticed an awful smell. One guy said what's that smell? Guy said I work for the circus that's in town and clean up after horses and elephants and I shower but the smell is in my pores. Other said why don't you get another job" Guy said "And quit show business?

Power often isn't usually about show friendship, it's about show business and often personal, yet it is wise for me not to take forceful aggressive people personal including myself. Yes sometimes aggression is personal and putting another on notice is necessary.

I'm not trying to advise you on what power is or isn't Okay? Your discernment. I find a lot of power in not knowing very often. Good news and relief to be a recovering know it all.

Hypocrisy best not be wholly detested. Nobody is perfect.

Will inject some humor in this heavy topic okay?

Power can bring vulnerability into my life. So power can be dangerous in the wrong hands including mine.

When I resist I have more of what I don't want. I'm arguing with the mirror, pissing in the wind, thinking off. Any thoughts please?

When I react I am giving away power.

Shocking quote by Elvis. "When things go Wrong don't go with them." Powerful statement, will leave it to you to discern.

Drunk walked out of bar, got into his car, steering wheel missing. Called police on his cell, they came asked what the problem? He said someone stole my steering wheel. Police said, Sir you sitting in the back seat!

Maybe I have the ability to change how I see power sometimes and other times I don't. It's fun to experiment as a hobby, and at least have a good At Bat.

I have to free to some degree to access power. Freedom is expensive said Martin Luther King Jr, and can be just another word for nothing left to lose.

I like opting to create rather than react. I lose power when I try to force reality, maintain when creative or don't know.

When I react, I'm like a pinball in a pinball machine, being knocked around randomly. Or like a cue ball when hit playing pool. Is there power in options of creation? Sometimes, at least a good at bat. If baseball player make's pitcher throw 12 pitches and strikes out still good at bat. Pitcher usually only has 110 pitches. This book will be full of paradox's. Many don't like paradox of progress because seems like every time I solve a problem I create another. That's okay for me, the perfection is in the progress.

Many situations are Beyond my pay grade as a human being. That's powerful to know that. It's nice to not have to pretend, I'm tired of pretending. How about you?

I like keeping lessons and flushing disappointments. One lesson I learned being associated with the famous McKinsey Group. "There is nothing as useless as doing something efficiently that doesn't need to be done at all." OMG that saves lots of energy and power struggles with know it all's like me.

Love Emerson, he says "To laugh often, to win the respect of people and affection of children, appreciation of honest critics, to endure betrayal, to find best in others, leave the world a better place daily if possible, to know one person has breathed easier because you have lived." That's power to me.

This book is really about the Intimacy of Power. If you recall force isn't intimate. Intimacy is about the Familiar,

Power is open. Force is closed, only gives info on a need to know basis.

Powerful people have a moral compass.

To be beholden first to lobbyists who didn't elect is to be a bottom feeder.

about being Vulnerable, about Boundaries that reflect Values. I rarely value the valueless am getting younger in the overall process.

Life is happening for me rather than to me most of the time. Ironically 1% is often enough. This comes from Honda, who said, Success is 99% failure. Wouldn't work for a Doctor, yet I like it.

Loneliness can be conquered by those who can bear solitude says Tillich. I like solitude not loneliness.

Sometimes what I don't know can't worry me. I ask less questions as I get younger and try to stay out of the Indispensable Middle.

Intimacy with money is not with people, remember I'm a capitalist. A homeless person maybe more intimate that a billionaire? What say you?

Notice I write in bullet fashion, like a pinball machine. The only time I want to look back is to see how far I've come. Yes and I've gone from Wild to Mild. I'm a journalist not a writer.

My thinking was distorted all the time. I tried to force solutions, then became more disturbed. I was disturbed because I was disturbable. I claim progress. Progress is a paradox because new challenges come to life as I meet and process old ones.

Few people ask my opinion, like our President or Supreme Court or Sports Managers or Wall St. Yet I have views and contribute by realizing, Nobody is Perfect. Like the Billionaire who got caught recently in a cheap massage parlor whore house. Not a happy ending. Poor ROI, return on investment.

I love Process trumps goals. The perfection is in the process. Many paradox's in power, like turning the other cheek and forgiveness. When I forgive I'm forgiven, yet I'm not the Source of forgiveness. Forgive AS.

For me there is no trouble so grave or great that cannot be mitigated by a nice cup of tea. Over simple yes, but works for me.

This is not a Designated Culprit book. Someone said, "Criticism is usually related to a loss of control, especially at myself." I like the idea intelligent people have plans, wise people have principles. I like Lighthouse Principles. Short story later about that. Displaced anger is a loss of power.

I won't define power, it's subjective in my experience. The basic premise of all questions is, if I say it you doubt it. If you say it it's true.

For me power will never intentionally harm anyone, including myself. Mercy is mightiest in the mightiest. I try to be under that kind of influence. Really an aggregate of influences.

Again, best not look back unless to see how far you have come. That's power for me.

My hope is this book will allow you the power to be younger if you're interested? Power ages people. Look at any President of the U S after four or 8 years. Most aged 3 times what normally would have. So was going up worth the coming down?

Stress is supposed to be healthy for me, its distress that ages faster than normal.

A Pyric victory is when I win the battle, lose the war. I like the idea of Peace and Intimacy. That doesn't mean a loss of power. I would have dropped the atomic bomb if I were Truman.

I've heard the CIA stands for Capitalism's Invisible Army. I think they had Kennedy killed, yet he made more enemies than any president I researched. Big difference in power and force. JFK allowed his brother RFK to force forces that were lethal. I'm a JFK fan wish he would have lived and his spirit does with many.

I'm not interested in shooting the messenger. They used to do that in Wild West when a piano player made a mistake. One put a sign on his piano, please don't shoot the piano player I'm doing the best I can.

I used to be different. Now I am the same. More alike than unalike. Gone from Wild to Mild. That's power for me.

I'm not the smartest or the dumbest, best or worst. Given up Est's and the claim to be special. That's power for me.

I love dialogue vs monologues. Everyone gets a vote with me, if you want one.

Here's Power? I cannot suffer in the past or future, they do not exist, and Einstein proved that. What I am suffering is my memory and imagination. Some give up drinking alcohol because it interferes with their suffering. Okay with me. Everyone is as right as me.

There's Power in being wrong. Letting professionals help when challenges beyond my pay grade which is amateur human being.

Reacting loses power for me, responding is freedom, allows options. Givers best set limits because takers rarely do. Okay to give and take. Do I still react? Yes but not as often.

Mark Twain said if you don't read the newspaper you're uninformed. If you do you're misinformed. Yet I like to keep up.

I believe the news media stokes fears to keep me watching what's 95% fake. Like the the North Korea nut, we have thousands of missiles, he threatened he wants one. Both North Korea and Iran know if they launched their country would be history.

When God was a Woman civilization was more civil. Glad that's happening again in my opinion.

Many believe war is a racket, especially since the robber barons of United States get our government to protect their interests. Ford, GE etc. did business with Hitler, then sued USA and won after war for bombing interests in Germany.

Exporting democracy when we aren't a democracy is fun for the powers that be. My Dad who was in most of WWII in Navy then Army said, war is started by old men with vested interests. Dick Chaney good example. Yes, Hitler had to be stopped and Stalin.

However, how is it we always have to have an enemy or bad guy? Starts Democrats Enemy Republicans and vice versa. Other always wrong is fake news. Fake power struggles my opinion.

How did Stephen Hawking die? Power outage. I will die physically, not spiritually, in fact get to be younger at heart.

I'm not a Christian, but Christ's comment to Pilot, you have no power over me unless my Father gives it to you, may be one of the most powerful statements in history.

Happiness comes and goes, principles stay. (If you don't like my principles I have others. —Groucho Marx

*For me happiness or unhappiness is not the point. One point for me is "How do I meet the problems I Face?
Bill Wilson Esq*

Friends with history are precious, the gift that keeps giving and rarely ask anything of each other. Bill Hale.

I wondered why somebody didn't do something-then I realized I am somebody. John Cashen.

Chapter 1:
Wall St. Federal Reserve, Religions

Wall St. was called Banksters after the depression. Interesting only planes flying in US for 72 hours after 911 were Bin Laden's relations going home. They did lots of business with Bushes.

Supposedly FDR saved capitalism from the capitalist's. Any thoughts?

FDR said, in politics nothing happens accidently. Many think he took the big aircraft carriers and fast battleships out of Pearl Harbor a month before the bombing by Japan. What say you?

There are Estates or Powers in our United States, usually 4 or less. They used to be called Clergy, Noble, Common. Then some called Executive, Judicial, Legislative, Federal Reserve and Media and Generic.

I believe in Media information, yet feel it causes chaos often by in sensationalism, stay tuned drama. That's called yellow journalism to keep people coming back. I don't buy, it's a poor return on my investment and not good for my health. I can't imagine how Rush Limbaugh

I Whisper a lot in this book. A good author whispers.

Serenity is not freedom from storms, its peace amidst storms?

stays alive with the poison he spews. Yet he laughs all the way to the bank.

1. For me power is Source, my higher powers that are non-preferential.

2. Is health, spiritually, physically, emotional? Like a three legged stool in balance as much as possible with a Village of Help.

3. Improv, meaning humor that isn't scripted yet lighthearted. I love like the new jokes and old like "Why the long face?"

Power is ambiguous. There is everyday power, defined as Clout or Influence or Juice. Then there is Elite Power meaning Dominance that serves only its own interests, like Hitler. Wall St. Federal Reserve, Politicians, Corporations. I understand investors' money is at risk. I'm a capitalist on a win-win basis or no deal.

History shows dictators collapse, but wreak havoc in the interim. Elite power meaning to me the people who make the snow balls and have others throw them. They don't always agree with each other. The Wizard of Oz had a lot of power until the curtain was lifted.

Scary times in my lifetime. 1944, FDR let powers that be take Henry Wallace off the ticket as Vice President. 80 % of American's wanted him on ticket. 2% wanted Harry Truman, Senator from Missouri. Truman was nominated. I liked Truman.

Some humor. Student asked Rabbi, why do all of you Rabbi's answer our questions with a question? Rabbi said " So how should we answer?"

Oliver Stone says the same dark powers that got rid of Wallace in 44 got rid of Kennedy in 63. I don't seem to be able to zero in on who those powers are, not doubt aggregate. Scary, one thing for sure, life is cheap to those alleged humans.

Again, I've heard the CIA can stand for Capitalism's Invisible Army. Yet it the powers behind them that make the snowballs in my opinion. Captains and Kings the fictional novel comes close to this sinister reality. I have no doubt Allen Dulles was directly behind Kennedys murder. Interesting Dulles died a horrible long death. So nobody gets away with anything in my experience. I love Emerson's essay on Compensation.

Having said that I don't want to invest in that Abyss. This book hopefully will suggest you have some options. Maybe 4. 1. Yes. 2. No. 3. Yes and No. 4. Only don't know. That's Power.

I don't believe my life is to be carried like a ball and chain. Light Hearted is my preference, except when sadness is in order. Yet I'm skeptical of bliss positive fake it till you make it advice. There is good and bad advice. Honesty is the best policy can get you killed. If I look into the abyss to much the abyss will look into me. Look at history back to Socrates, JFK, etc.

When I'm always faking it till I make it I'm pretending most of the time.When do I have time to enjoy life?

Am I too perfect for this world? (used to be).

Kid who was forced to play sports after loss of big game. "You don't see me crying."

If I'm not good enough without the Gold Medal, I won't be good enough with it.

I like Gary Zukav's, Seat of the Soul. He says, "Every action, thought, and feeling is motivated by intention, and that intention is a cause that exists as one with an effect. If I participate in the cause, it's not possible not to participate in the effect." So it's humbling to opt for the effects I want to create and produce. One powerful humble option is I don't know. I use that often.

There is power in being powerless. In fact power and powerlessness are two sides of one coin in my experience. I hang out with the powerless most of the time and enjoy observing without being invested in toxic dangerous power. I have not always been so impartial and have been drunk with power and got right sized by reality. Good news is sometimes I have been lifted up and humanized not always humiliated.

There is Power in Humility, defined for me as Earthy, Open, Young at Heart, often Only Don't Know a Buddhist Principle.

Power is willing for me. Force is willful. I have options. Yet I believe in the "Reality of not having all the answers or questions."

Big difference in Power vs. Force. One person interviewed said they are the same. I respectfully disagree. Force equals counter-force. What I resist persists. Too much wear and tear for me, even if I get what I want, the price is too high. Reminds me of The Lie of the High. ROI to high even if I get what I want. What say you?

Some feel sex is power. Henry Kissenger said-power is an aphrodisiac. Yes, but to me that attracts the wrong kind of person, a co-dependent looking for a parent child relationship. Step 13, please hook up with me and share my unmanageable life, since I have an intimacy disorder.

Again, I like lighthouse principles.

Hope the ROI, (return on investment) is healthy for you. Trump won the presidency because they watched the ROI in the Electoral College states.

Robert Kennedy said in 1968. "I found out something I never knew. I found out that my world was not the real world." Powerful, Humble statement. Wish he would have found that reality sooner.

Hope this work will offer you some real options you may or may not know you have. I try not to carry life around like a ball and chain. I have a brother, (2 sisters, and 6 brothers) who is a professor, he asks his students if they ever read anywhere that life is supposed to be easy? No one yet has given him an answer that was factual.

Power is relative and limited in my experience. Turning on a light switch is a humbling experience. I participate, yet I'm not source.

Those who serve, rule. There are exceptions. What say you?

Same with oxygen etc. Good news is I have Access via the freedom of Options.

If I don't believe in magic, it can't find me. What's magic. I have or have access to anything I want. Oh My.

Yes I have choices, it's okay to make mistakes. People who aren't doing much don't make many mistakes. What say you?

I like power with others not power or force over. I will stop and ask your opinion often by asking "What say you?" Okay? I like dialogues not monologues.

My granddaughter Grace, 13 said power is good unless it's in the wrong hands. Wow, homerun over the center field wall, Grace.

Trusted friend of mine says power is ability. The ability to affect or at least the attempt. The E for Effort is always a good at bat.

Interesting that women in USA couldn't vote until 100 years ago. Point most woman's DNA proves to not be as aggressive as men. Most women wouldn't send their son or daughter to a political war like Vietnam or Iraq. This DNA is changing and becoming Civilized and balance with time. Too bad we didn't have the first woman president recently.

Yet history says women used to be Goddesses, men were gofers. Until men created the devil and convinced woman since they were stronger physically, woman needed their protection. I really believe civilization has progressed for years because of civil men and woman. We all have female and male chromosome's thanks for the Powers that be.

Let's discuss Religions Okay. The big three now are Christianity, Islam and Hindu's. All have a long, long history of abuses sexually of woman and children.

The good news is today you will be arrested and criminally charged if you abuse someone or if you cover it up. Being sick mentally does not allow a pass on consequences or let you be above the law. Yes no excuses for predators or those who cover up. The Catholic Church finds itself humiliated and embarrassed because it keeps better records than the other big religions. Forgiveness does not trump our Laws, Thank God. I still believe in Tender Mercy and correction rather than demonizing sick people, yet they can't be allowed to run rampant.

As a Catholic my relationship is with God and Community first before our institution.

I would love your feelings pro and con on this heartbreaking history?

There are two mistakes, interfering with another or my growth.

You don't always get what you want, but if you try you might just get what you need. —Bob Dylan

The highest form of Wisdom is Kindness. —The Talmud

There are those who bet love come's but once and yet, I'm oh so glad we met the second time around or 3rd or however many necessary.

Buddha says, life is suffering and when I accept that reality I still suffer, yet not as much.

Chapter 2:
Is Civilization Working?

I Love Steven Pinkers book Better Angels of our Nature. Shows civilization is working. Two reasons, most people care about each other, even strangers AS themselves. Second, most woman are more civil than most men.

Violence is decreasing per capita worldwide as is poverty etc. Per capital is key. It is spiking in some areas. Won't see that on evening news that rarely has time for good news. Put the drama junkies in rehab. Fake news is about staying tuned to terror. Yes it's good to know what's going on, but the whole world isn't going up in flames.

I believe that Rest in Peace is for the Living. Yet I'm born every morning and die each night and try to live each day as a life. Practice helps. Process trumps goals, the perfection is in the process for me.

I love the idea "if you want to save the world, make your bed in the morning." That may be where my power begins and ends some days, after saying please in the morning and thanks at night.

*Nodding the head doesn't row the boat.
Irish proverb.*

Asked a lady if she was always in such a good mood? She said I hope so. Wow, good moods are contagious. Yet I don't want to be around perpetually smiling people. I'm more apt to be around those not pretending and honestly sad and able to express their feelings regardless of their situation.

Chapter 2

Guy walked into Tavern Restaurant, no one at the bar expect bartender and monkey at the end. He ordered a shot of whiskey and glass of beer. Bartender gave, said excuse me have to go to restroom. He drank shot, half of glass of beer, looked over at Restaurant side people eating dancing to music of trio. He heard something turned around and the monkey was pissing in his beer. He went to guy leading trio and said, do you know a monkey just pissed in my beer? Trio leader said no, but if you hum a few bar we will try and play it. This is not a heavy book, yet I won't duck history or reality.

Some say the color of truth is gray, McGeorge Bundy said that. I don't feel it's black or white or gray. I don't believe in The Truth but aggregate truths, a truth rather than the truth. You always get a vote with me.

Yet, our Government, Wall St, Media etc. can be "Lying Machines," I'm a capitalist and a patriot, I understand the difference in Show Business and Show Friendship. Studies show people lie over 50 times every day to ourselves and others. Point? Nobody is perfect.

So you're either at the table or on the menu. Nice option for me is neither. If a game is rigged I can opt not play and walk away.

While this book is not holier than thou, I know some of the most sinister stuff has happened in our Country like JFK being killed. A great book on this the Devils Chessboard by David Talbot.

One of the most beautiful experiences is the Mysterious. —Albert Einstein.

The very pursuit of happiness, thwarts happiness. —Victor Frankl

Chapter 2

I like to talk and write like I'm correct and listen like I'm incorrect or wrong. That leaves tons of room for how you feel. I love dialogues rather than monologues.

How can this book demonstrate a little power by saving you and me money and give some new power?

One quick way if you're a homeowner. Insurance companies raise your premiums every year based on Restoration value versus market value. Who's in charge of the Butter? Not you. Most people make house payments to mortgage companies and don't know this.

Point, last year I saved about $400 shopping and opting for market value, you can too. If my home got destroyed I could elect not to rebuild and sell the lot or find someone reputable to rebuild probably lower than market value. So why throw way money?

Another challenge, real estate taxes in your county. I know a woman who challenges and wins every year, again saving hundreds of dollars. That's power.

Do you or I have any power, any options, and any freedom? Yes and no, it varies daily.

My one hope for you this book may allow you to be a bit younger no matter what you age, with power options.

Picasso was asked at 95, why his paintings were deep colors and dull when he first started painting and are light and colorful now. He said "It takes a long time to become young!" I would add it takes a long time to know who is in charge of the butter.

This book is not meant to be heavy in fact this book is Improv. Improv in comedy is Ad Lib, agree then respond.

Horse walked into a bar, the bartender ask "Why the long face?"

It's not if it bleeds it leads. Some powers that be are healing and necessary for our Civilization Process. I like the Perfection and Power is in the Process.

Progress does come with a cost, simple yet not easy. I like Process and power, trumps goals.

Favorite true story. Bill Bradley, All American Basketball player, Rhodes Scholar, Pro Basketball Star, Senator, was at roost for him. Waiter served rolls and pat of butter before lunch. Bradley used his pat and asked for another. Waiter say sorry one pat to a person. Bradley said this roost is for me, do you know who I am? Waiter said no I don't. Do you know who I am? Bradley said no. Waiter said I'm the man in charge of the butter.

Point? I'm going to run into many situations where I'm not in charge of the butter, no matter how much power I have, I'm cornered.

So shall I have a power struggle, walk away or pause and step back? Sometimes I'm Summarily beached like a whale.

So shall I have power struggles or step back and pause or react like a pin ball? Works when one can remember. Doesn't when lightning in bottle.

Is there sometimes Power in being Powerless, in turning the other cheek? Yes, but not always.

Second favorite true story. Navy destroyer on night duty, it's foggy. Sees another light, says change course we are on a collision course. Response from light, you change

There's more to life than being happy. Happiness for me is a by-product and ensues.

Everything can be take from a person but there right to perspective. The freedom to opt for your music, your drummer, your life, your Navajo Peace is priceless in my experience.

course. Destroyer Captain says I'm a destroyer and I'm captain you change course. Response, I'm a Corporal and a Lighthouse.

Yes sometimes best to change course no matter how powerful.

Bill Martin head of Federal Reserve said Feds job is take away punch bowl when party getting out of hand. Too bad Fed doesn't believe that anymore in my opinion. But no one ask my opinion, so I punt.

Can I be making progress and not feel it? Yes I can and reality is often friendlier than I experience. Begs the question, are happy people happy all the time? Is happiness the point of life? Again, feelings are never wrong, but often inaccurate.

One point for me is, how do I face the challenges I meet?

I have never read anywhere that life is supposed to be easy. Worth living overall, yet not easy. Buddha says when accept life is not easy, then it not as hard. That's one Paradox of Power and there are many.

When Power vs Force, power usually wins, historically. Like Iraq, it was invaded by force and created the Taliban and Isis. The Power of the terrorist is fading, yet was created by Force.

I believe a Terrorist is one without a sense of Humor. So I'm a recovering terrorist.

The Civilization Process a concept written about by Steven Pinker in a book, "The Better Angels of our

Nature," says per capita for thousands of years humans are and continue to be progressively Civil. Violence is down worldwide per capita, so is poverty, addictions, divorces, teen pregnancies. etc. This isn't selling news, apparently most people like to stay tuned for drama or conflict. Maybe that makes one feel grateful that their life is Civil. I don't know or pretend to know. I like everyone has a vote or right to their own music or cup of Tea.

That process included two principles. One humans in general are compassionate and have each other's back more often. Two Woman are less aggressive via DNA and most woman would never send their son or daughter to a dumb political war, like Iraq or Vietnam.

Science shows men are getting less hostile and macho as another reason Civilization can claim progress.

None of this ignores reality like mass shooting in Vegas or schools.

You will rarely see in the media that violence is down per capita worldwide. Yes it's spiking in some areas, yet down worldwide as is poverty, inequality etc. Good news doesn't sell.

This book isn't about positive thinking or I'm right your wrong, power struggles or monologues. I like dialogues where each have a vote, not monologues where people talk past each other.

Dialogues are work, simple yet not easy. I love Rabbi Martin Buber who in the 1940s wrote about dialogue in his classic book I-Thou.

I "Get to" dialogue with Reality, our Universe and my own consciousness in many ways. Being Still, writing, with others.

I like to write and communicate like I'm right listen like I'm wrong, because I'm often wrong about my best interests and no doubt often have no idea what's in your best interests.

Some of what I feel is a truth not the truth and may be uncomfortable for me or you. I have no patent on the truth or your comfort.

Some day if I'm in court and asked to swear to tell the truth, the whole truth and nothing but the truth, I would like to ask "what is the truth," then ask the judge and lawyers to swear to the same oath?

I feel the truth is subjective and you have a vote and right to decide. I would probably get sentenced for contempt. The powers in court often ignore our Rights of Freedom of Expression. I'm not a lawyer, yet can read the law. I believe the law is necessary yet first and foremost a business. Judge Oliver Wendell Holmes said to a lawyer complaining his client wasn't getting justice. This is a court of Laws not of justice. Wow that's power.

What do I want? Justice. When do I want it Now! I don't believe anyone gets away with anything, right or wrong. So there is Justice and Cause and Effect.

I'm picking up good vibrations. Sometimes it's best for me to lower vibrations.

Nice freedom not to be a threat to me or you. I'm a safe person, this wasn't always true in my mental illness.

Tears have both bitter and sweet chemicals. Both are healing.

Grasshopper hoped in tavern, bartender said hi, we have a drink named after you, would you like one? Grasshopper said, Oh you have a drink named Irving?

Is someone pissing in your drink?

I have interviewed many people for this book and your feelings about Power are valuable, please send them to me and I will include in the second edition.

You are sincerely invited to vote in this offering and agree, disagree or don't know or care, okay? I will often stop often and ask "What say you?" I can be reached at maudley3@aol.com or 913-375-7290.

Chapter 3:
Bottom Feeders?

Two billionaires got arrested in Florida in Feb of 2019 along with a bunch of other powerful guys. Wonder why these wealthy guys had no relationship with Intimacy. A Prostitute female or male can't teach anything about Intimacy because being close and vulnerable takes time and sharing feelings. I wish you and yours Intimacy and wish that asset for the Johns who got caught and the Prostitutes, both bottom feeders in my experience.

I have experienced an Intimacy Disorder and am glad to report recovered and recovering. It's healthy for me to be intimate with Reality even if cynical. Processing feelings, darkness to light for me does not have cause and effect upside-down. Yet wise for me not to look into the abyss to long and stay lighthearted unless appropriate. I love C. S. Lewis, he says "I didn't know grief felt like fear." So does sadness for me. Good to process. Writing helps for me. Carrying unnecessary baggage interferes with the quality of my life and quality of being Surrendered.

Devil walked into mass, priest and altar boys and parishioners all ran out doors, except one old guy. Devil asked why aren't you afraid of me like the others. Guy

What is life expecting from me. It's good to have hopes and expectations, yet for me, "It's what is life expecting from me?" —Victor Frankl

Friendship may well be reckoned the masterpiece of Nature. —Emerson.

Criticism is always a sever loss of control.

said, why should I be afraid of you, I've been married to your sister for 30 years.

Bottom feeders are those who take or try take advantage of people in distress. Like try to steal your home or you being foreclosed on for an unfair price.

So what. I like the idea you can't cheat an honest person. But I can cheat a person in distress. Yet I'm really cheating myself and I believe nobody gets away with anything. When I help you I help me, when I cheat you I cheat me. Immediate cause and effect even if I don't experience it.

In sports, especially professional, owner cheat the fans by controlling the refs in my opinion, same in college. So what? Many know that yet go for entertainment. Most coaches know and many players. That's show business not show friendship. Does truth set me free or piss me off? What say you?

Fake news is to get most people to stay tuned. Rarely see anything healthy on news, 99 % if bleeds it leads. That's bottom feeding and fear mongering, yet I have options. Our president was the first one to call out media on fake news. Now he is King of Fake news in my opinion. Not a problem for me. I try to respect any President.

I don't respect most politicians. They look you right in the eye and lie and have fun doing it. Off with their heads. Yet they aren't getting away with anything in my opinion.

Most politicians are bottom feeders except at election time. Do they really represent us first or the lobbyists who sent them on expensive vacations and contribute to them? Throw the incumbent's out, monitor the new, and throw them out if at the trough. Not going to happen, yet divests me.

I don't believe a Republic is a Democracy. Yet I'm free to put the Canary in the Coal Mine and see if it dies or lives.

Many top feeders in life. Yet don't hear of. Do you know the poor give more to the poor than wealthy? Who is really rich or poor? What say you?

Chapter 4:
Who's On First?

Of course from Abbot and Costello. You younger people can Utube. I will never find out who is on first, because who is on first. Often power is right under my nose. I can be sitting on a box of gold and not know it. Defining power and gold for you is very important. If I say it (define it) you doubt it. If you say it, it's true. That is the premise of all questions. Most successful sales people live by that principle.

Influence is an interesting word. What influence are you under? Many feel they have to take drugs to be powerful, when in fact drugs disempower.

Being under the influence of power can be fun or abusive. I can and have been drunk on power. That comes with a hangover can cause some to commit suicide trying to get power back. Victory and defeat are temporary. In Rome after a victory they put the Conqueror in a chariot and they circled the area for cheers. A slave stood behind the man and whispered, victory is temporary. I would add so is defeat.

I like a Hasidic quote. The wheel of fortune. There are two kinds of fools, the fool on top of the wheel who never thinks they will be one the bottom again, and the fool on the bottom of the wheel who never thinks they will be on top again. I like the middle, the ordinary and giving up the claim to be special on top or bottom. What say You?

Again, I cannot suffer from the past or future because they do not exist. What I suffer from is memory and imagination.

In Scott Peck's classic, The Road Less Traveled, he starts out, Life is Difficult. When I accept that life is difficult it's a paradox that it's not as difficult. I try to remember that principle often. What say You?

Again, the media frequently compounds a problem to get me to stay tuned. No way will I be manipulated that way. I like Win-Win transactions.

Yes there are Innocent Victims, news helps us help others. It's easy to get stuck in I'm beyond my Sister and Brother's Keeper.

I love a metaphor a good friend of my created. It's called the Relationship Hat. Red hat is, you're not meeting my expectations, go to jail. Black hat is, look what you did to me for not meeting your expectations, (that I didn't agree on) I'm a victim and in your jail.

Third is the White hat, my sister and brother's keeper. The absence of red and black, even though I can't connect

Chapter 4

I am responsible for the well being of others and myself. I'm responsible to Civilization. Takes a village.

What I resist persists. —Carl Jung

They who are not busy being born, are busy dying. —Bob Dylan

the dots. I accept nobody is perfect and let peace and forgiveness begin with me.

The Relationship Hat principle, De-triangle's me progressively, from strife and toxic relating with life others and myself. Take that to the bank.

Back to Force. When our government soldiers and civilians die, even when the Best and Brightest are in charge.

I love "never cut a knot you can untie."

Chapter 5:
JFK

I love and loved JFK, was only 20 when he got elected. His eyes shined when he looked at people. Wasn't perfect. Made more enemies that any president ever.

That cost him and his brother's his life. I come from a big competitive family of 9 like the Kennedys.

Went to confession recently and confessed I compete with everyone, God, others, even myself. Priest said "What you too?" The good news is I claim progress and don't compete (have power struggles) AS much. What a relief. People have the right to their own drummer and music and are AS right as me ever if we disagree 100%. A healthy option for me is to agree to disagree. That isn't always possible, yet is more often than not.

It's healthy for me to minimize power struggles with Life—Other's and Myself.

C. S. Lewis said "What you too, I thought I was the only one?" That's the beginning of power for me and often friendship and Intimacy.

All bleeding stops. ER concept by doctors.

Life is hard, not just to love but to grasp.
—Bob Dylan

The Ambiguity of Reality of the answer is blowing in the wind.

Chapter 5

I come from a big family of Catholics of 9 like the Kennedys. Competition was rampant, with each other, authority, sports. We didn't know it yet we were in competition with ourselves. Today they called it OCD, obsessive compulsive disorder. Some of that is an asset. Yet I believe it got 4 or 5 of the 9 Kennedys killed.

I love Lincoln. He said if I had six hours to cut down a tree, I would spend four sharpening the saw.

I like a metaphor called A Three Legged Stool, mental, physical, and spiritual. Love the idea I don't have all the answers for me or you or the questions. Your music, cup of tea, drummer.

What is the lesson in a rough experience? Learn it accept it move on. Not always that simple or easy. An insight came to me recently, 12 years after a wild experience. Again, I've gone from Wild to Mild. Mild allows me not to miss anything. What say you?

The Kennedys have gone from Wild to Mild. John Jr, was skiing with the clan when about 12, had an accident was crying. RFK came along said Kennedys don't cry. John Jr, said, "this one does."

Remember, if I say it, you doubt it. If you say it, it's true.

I love feel to heal and heal to feel. I know feelings are fickle, yet what's in my heart is the quickest way to reality for me. Yet I caution about advice is often the worst vice. What's good for me can be poison for you.

I used to be different. Now I'm the same. Meaning more alike than not. Nobody is perfect. Wants never run out, so I can exhaust myself seeking and seeking and seeking.

I don't feel I'm better or worse than anyone AS much as I used to. I was never the same usually better. Now I'm more alike than unalike most humans.

What about terrorists? No not same. Yet I like a terrorist is one without a sense of humor. So sometimes I'm a terrorist. I know sometimes it's appropriate to be sad.

It used to be easier for me to be angry than sad. Not anymore. Carrying that sadness like a ball and chain is unnecessary. I have options and have had lots of help ejecting baggage.

Love the idea "Structure binds anxiety and fears are educated into me and most unhealthy fears can be educated out .

Progressively. The perfection is in the process and paradoxes.

Process trumps goals. Goals immediately separate me.

I like breathing the same air, bleeding when cut, crying when hurt, and holding good feelings for everyone.

Yes and terrorist is one without a sense of humor.

Chapter 5

Arrogance swims upstream and ultimately dies of exhaustion. Humility and gratitude flows with the river of life into multiple safe secure coves and inlets and recycles and recirculates the rough waves. Bill Hale.

The Marques's of Queenberry rules do not apply with forceful groups or people. It's a Zero sum game.

I wondered why somebody didn't do something-then I realized I am somebody. —John Cashen

Good to be busy being born than busy dying. —Bob Dylan

Freedom is not having to look for the next high.

Chapter 6:

Drunk on Power or Force? What Influences Am I Under?

Sometimes a cigar is just a cigar, Freud said.

Yes, being drunk on power for me usually isn't seen until a hindsight reflection. Hindsight is 20/20 most of the time, not all of the time.

Humility comes into this matter. Most of the real powerful people I meet are humble, earthy, open, teachable, and humorous and are good at what comedians call Improv. Improv, that takes two and the premise comes of Yes and. I respond to whatever the other says with the agreement of Yes and. If the other says, you are rotten sob. I say Yes and are you just finding that out?

I can be or get drunk on Willfulness, forcing a matter rather than trying to dialogue and get a win win result. Drunk on Power does not give others a vote. You're invisible, no vote, and an object. When I objectify you I objectify me.

I like to step back and ask myself, What Influence am I Under?

1. Reality and Hope.

2. Fellowship of Spirit.

3. Lighthouse principles.

4. Non-Preferences Divinity-Source.

5. Three Legged Stool.

6. Family- extended, strangers haven't met.

7. Solitude, music, reading, cup of tea.

8. Born-Die daily.

9. Play ball where is vs. wish. Bobby Jones.

10. You too, thought I was the only one. CSL.

11. Improv.

12. What does life expect from me?

Freud said, The Irish are the only people impervious to psychotherapy. (I think he was an wanna be Irish.)

Like the wealthy powerful guys that got caught in the sting with the prostitutes. They all were objectifying each other, meaning the prostitutes and men.

Sure was love while it lasted. Is it easier to get angry than experience sadness? Was for me. It very important for me not to carry life like a ball and chain. Sufficient is the day....What say you?

Chapter 6

Non-Negativity is balance. —Martin Seligman

Four word Ice breaker. Tell me about yourself?

Success in 99% failure. —Honda

Truck stuck under bridge. Kid 10 watched for 2 hours while fireman, police etc. tried to free.

Finally said, "How about letting some air out of the tires?"

---

100 years old's birthday, never flew in airplane. Friend had a friend take up piper cub. When landed pilot said, did you enjoy? 100 year old said, yes, "but I never put all my weight down."

Point. It's selfish not to ask for help. I like acronym for FEAR= Find Every Available Resource. It's take a village.

Your feelings please? Is it, Sometimes it's good to have a Heart to Heart?

This is my 10th book. I write to process and redirect. I heard the opposite of depression is expression. I'm rarely depressed, do not like being high or low.

Again, favorite quote. We finally found a thrill for the person who no longer seems thrillable. The Ordinary. Works for me.

Chapter 7:
Mendacity and Sulpher. NFL-NCAA

Love this true FDR story. Eleanor with in Oval office with President. He had three cabinet meeting waiting to give him opinions on sensitive issue. Wife said I will leave, he said no stay.

First guy gave opinion, FDR said thanks, your absolutely right. Eleanor was shocked, knew FDR felt differently.

Second guy gave opinion different first. FDR said thanks, your absolutely right.

Third different from one and two. FDR said thanks, your absolutely right.

Eleanor said unbelievable, unprincipled, and hypocritical. I thought I knew you but I am wrong.

FDR said Eleanor, your absolutely right.

Everyone is absolutely right.

Nobody absolutely has to do anything.

Are there consequences and compensations?

Can I be passionately in love with suffering?

So some stop using addictions because they interfere with their suffering?

Point, everyone is absolutely right and feel 100% right. Problem is being right can be a form of violence that is a monologue that objectifies and doesn't allow others to have a vote. That's not real power in my experience.

I love the Premise of all questions is, if I say it you doubt it. If you say it, it's true. What say you?

NFL-NCAA, how much Refs make? Who cares how much refs make. Am I jealous? I was shocked to learn years ago how big business the NCAA is. That is changing, they fined KU's Coach Mangino for complaining about a flagrant bad call. He got fined $10,000 dollars for complaining about a call that 50,000 people saw and millions on TV. Zero humility. However times are changing.

Same of NFL, in front of 80,000 people and millions on TV. Show business, not show friendship. You have the power of being entertained. If you think the field is level that's how you feel.

I have three daughters, four sons, 11 grandchildren.

One daughter Kellie won every track race she ran in high school, was State Champion of Kansas cross country 2 mile. All champs in race, Kellie won by about 75 yards. She used let friends win sometime in Jr High, coach didn't agree. Kellie knew we don't have to win them all in life. In fact some of the best lessons from losses.

It's okay to have a fling with life--a trip to to moon on gossamer wings.

When I'm not good enough without what I want, I won't be good enough with.

Best plans of mice and men often go awry. Process trumps plans.

Mendacity and Sulphur can be entertaining.

Chapter 8:
Are Addictions a pitiful attempt at Self-Medication

Yes and millions have recovered and are recovering from addictions to both Drugs and Process addictions. Process addictions are bulimia, gambling, workaholics etc. They are really getting chemicals from the chemical factory between their ears. I contend I can get drunk on willfulness, self will run riot, instincts on rampage. Force vs Power.

Hindsight has shown me The Lie of The High. The only high I got was the high price of suicidal depressions. I hung out in low places mentally and physically, with peers of my ILK.

Like a drink of alcohol the effect wears off and another is necessary. The cycle is Chasing False Highs and Running for Lows. I wrote a book with that title in 2011. It's on Amazon Kindle if you want a free excerpt.

The rush of battle if often a potent and lethal addiction, for war is a drug. (with myself, others or life.)

Lincoln said, "I've been driven to my knees many times by the overwhelming conviction I had no place else to go."

Depression was a crucial part of the alleged high for me. The dopamine factor goes on, a cycle that many are unaware of. The high even if a strong spiritual experience is a bait and hook that one can chase all their life. I had two uncles that did. One died and 90 the other 91. Heartbreaking suffering via pitiful attempt at self-medication.

Is there a benefit from suffering? Can a person go past the point of having an option? I think so, but seems to have only one choice, to keep on self-medicating. Heartbreaking. Like being on auto pilot.

Notice the chapters are getting shorter?

Final bit of vulgar humor okay? Couple married had child. Dr. said say new, child has no torso. They took him home. Dr called on his birthday 10 years later, said good news, found a perfect torso match. Mom and Dad ran to his room said we have perfect birthday gift. Kid said, I hope it's not another damned hat. Oh My. When I say Oh My, my heart is light. Same with WTF?

I experience Natural Highs sometimes. I can't force them, yet they are as natural as our seasons. Come and go. I like Life gives us moments and for these moments we pay for with our life. I believe in Eternal Life with Fresh Daily Bread.

It's okay for me to be Stoic sometimes or not know how I feel about something.

What's your feelings?

Chapter 8

It's hard to stop dancing when the music is still playing.

There's more to life than power or force.

Can I detox from toxic drama?

Full Meaning of Love Neighbor AS yourself?

Leave a little of the Game of Life to Reality.

How long? Not long! —Martin Luther King Jr

Conclusions
What Do You Want?

I like the idea of trying to give people what they ask for if practical. They usually don't ask for much.

Simple I want justice. When do I want it? Now. You have your own wants and Justice and what you want is usually the same. Problem is Reality gets in the way.

Love the song "Can't Always Get What I Want." But if you try you just might get what you need.

I love Thoreau's quote "If a person does not keep pace with their companions, perhaps it is because they hear a different drummer. Let them step to the music they hear, however measured or far away. That's Power.

It has taken me a long time to become younger. The Prudent person thinks it more important that Fate has conceded more that it has denied. That's Power.

If I'm only contented when I'm getting what I want, as an adult I'm not going to be contented most of the time.

I love baseball it repairs our losses, says Walt Whitman.

I like--never cut a knot you can untie.

I like--no tickee, no laundry.

I like--Fake News is a way to keep people coming back and upset. Yellow journalism.

I like--if you coulda you woulda.

I love--Learn the Lesson and move on, carrying baggage is unnecessary. You option, possibly?

I love--never interfere with a winning streak, from movie Bull Durham. Respect the Streak.

Some final take a ways. Author if remember.

1. De-Traingling- get out of middle.
2. Be yourself, original worth more.
3. Issues people of goodwill disagree.
4. RIP=Rest In Peace is for the living.
5. What Influences are your under?
6. You are as right as I am.
7. No I without you. Martin Buber.
8. I guess you have your reasons.
9. Why hard to talk people claim know God?
10. Are you Velcro or Teflon?

---

11. First Wealth is Health.

12. Difference in broke and poor.

13. I miss 100% of shots I don't take.

14. Drama can be uninvited. No thanks.

15. I don't suffer in past or future.

16. I used to be different, now I'm the same.

17. Only high is high price for no life.

18. Sex has little to do with Intimacy.

19. Friends are the masterpiece of Nature.

20. The Emperor has no clothes.

———

21. Trust the process.

22. Process trumps goals.

23. Perfection is in the process.

24. Power as you Understood Power.

26. No advance praise for this book. It will ruin my autopsy. Mistakes were made. But now by me.

27. Reward: a job well done is having done it.

28. Buddha, what have you gained from meditation? Nothing lost a lot of Anger, Lust, Greed, Envy, Sloth, Gluttony, False Pride.

29. Sometimes a cigar is just a cigar. Freud.

30. How long? Not long. —Martin L King Jr

———

31. Murphy's law, if can go right will, if can go wrong will.

32. Half-measures avail us nothing.

33. Option, react - create or only don't know.

34. Finally found a thrill, the Ordinary.

35. When things don't add up-Subtract.

36. Only what I give do I possess.

37. Prescribe the symptom for addictions.

38. Two kinds of fools, fool on top- bottom.

39. The days of Dogma in Spirituality—over.

40. Way out is through.

---

41. When things go wrong don't go with them. Elvis.

42. Laughter is life's best gift, an instant vacation.

43. I see more when I slow down. Slow is Real,

44. Reality is how I relate with life.

45. The Power of the Quiet Ambivert.

46. When I'm happy for no reason, I bring happiness to my experiences, rather than trying to extract it from them. I live From Happiness, rather than For. Happiness is usually a by-product. It probably is temperament or glandular. It's not something that can be forced from life. So if you are reasonably happy, stop worrying and see what treasures you can pull from you own reality. Unhappiness starts by trying to be happier.

Conclusions

47. Happy people have no history. —Tolstoy.

48. I'm not waiting for anything to happen.

49. Politics is Theater. Fake News.

50. What Influences am I under?

---

51. Mortgage means "Death Grip."

52. Giving up Pretending is Freedom.

53. If I want to much, likely disappointed.

54. Simple not easy, a price must be paid.

55. I wish you and yours Enough. Irish Poem.

56. I must learn to see people in light of not do or don't do, but what they suffer.

57. Way I perceive others way I perceive me.

58. I'm responsible but not in charge.

59. Being sensitive can be a asset.

60. Nothing I despise in another is absent me

---

61. Help me forgive those who make different mistakes than I do.

62. You must have your reasons, your music.

63. I like alive peace not dead peace.

64. I drink of Spirit-not alcohol etc.

65. What you too? Thought I only one.

66. Learn the lesson-Drop disappointments.

67. I don't know who you think you are? But this isn't you. Mom to 19 year old in jail.

68. Some questions are best not asked.

69. No one can make your feel inferior without your consent. Eleanor Roosevelt.

70. I best not look to past or future for explanations or solutions.

---

71. Let there be spaces in your togetherness.

72. Help me avoid I know what's best for you. It's your music and drummer.

73. Intimate relationships cannot flourish under conditions of inequality or unfairness.

74. Those who don't believe in Magic will never find it.

75. Experience is a hard teacher. It give the test first and lesson after.

76. I like to dance not wrestle in relations.

77. Maybe out of Love, Faith and Hope, Hope is first?

78. Again, best not fuck with a winning streak or Good at Bats! I wish you Enough.

79. Some are alive only because it's against the law to kill them. Used to be one of these.

80. First rule of collaboration? Give up being right.

---

81. I've learned there are people who love me that don't know how to show love.

82. When I'm not able to accept present reality, I will still be discontented if reality changes.

83. What the Hell is Power?

84. Aware of Tender Mercy's is a big asset.

85. All isn't well, in general never better.

86. You've come far Pilgrim. It feels like far.

87. Yond Cassius has a lean and hungry look.

88. Please don't shoot the piano player, I'm doing the best I can.

89. Everyone has a plan, until they get hit in the mouth. Mike Tyson.

90. Problems don't age well. Solutions do.

---

91. Smooth seas do not make skillful sailors.

92. Christ only on cross three hours.

93. Angels fly, they take selves lightly.

94. Lemons to lemonade.

95. I introduce my elephants not yours.

96. I like models not critics.

97. Give each other room to be human.

98. Try not to bring everyone down.

99. Often I get cause and effect backwards.

100. Is this the hill I'm going to die on?

---

101. Well you know that's just your opinion man. The Dude Abides.

102. If competitor drowning, turn on a hose and stick it in their mouth.

103. Unhappy because of what's eating me.

104. Just another Bozo on the bus.

105. Et tu Brute? It's not that I love Caesar less, it's that I love Rome more.

106. Awareness of your Tender Mercies?

107. Maturing Intimate Relationship signs.

   a. Caring for each other.

   b. Humor.

   c. Honest communications.

   d. Common purposes.

   e. Equality.

   f. Sense of adventure.

   g. Some Shared experiences.

   h. Respect each other's feelings.

   i. Passion, healthy sex.

   j. Sharing domestic duties. From book Why Love is not Enough. Sol Gordon.

108. Life is difficult. Accept that and still difficult but no as. Scott Peck.

109. Service means what does life expect?

110. God's will? God as I understood wants for me what I want and willing to work for.

110 A. Please don't tell me what I want to hear.

---

111. Kings and Pawns go back in same box after game.

112. You will have bad times, but they will always wake up to the good times you have been missing. Robin Williams.

113. Structure binds unnecessary anxiety.

114. Only thing lacking in my life is what I'm not giving. Marianne Williamson.

115. It's exhausting to try to live two lives or to manage my life or other's or play God.

116. Isn't Life is hard enough without being exhausted?

117. I claim progress not perfection. Equal, no better or worse.

118. I like models not critics. Yet I can learn more critic's than models. Critic's wake me up. Like relationships are not here to make me happy or unhappy but to make me conscious. Eckhart Tolle.

119. What I bless blesses me, what I damn, damns me.

120. Dogs bark. People talk. Sometimes I have no off switch. Part of being human. Nobody is perfect. The perfection is in the process. Process trumps goals.

---

121. When half gods go, Gods arrive.

122. Playing fast and loose with advice can be tragic.

123. Yes I believe people have some autonomy, like different fingerprints.

124. Real power is not abused.

125. Power is not force. Not manipulative, not loud, not pretensive. Isn't pretending exhausting?

126. Power isn't fact, often a process.

127. Power for me is Tender Mercy.

128. Misery not only loves company, it insists on company.

129. My fresh daily bread is Enough, often awakens my youthful Spirit of Hope.

130. It's okay for me to experience my Dark Night of my Soul occasionally.

I'm a Dealer. A dealer in Hope.

Again, what's the best and worst advice you ever received?

What say you?

Conclusion: What Do You Want?

Conclusions, Part II
Hopefully Graceful Exits

I Whisper a lot in this book. A good author whispers.

Serenity is not freedom from storms, its peace amidst storms?

Am I too perfect for this world? (used to be).

Kid who was forced to play sports after loss of big game. "You don't see me crying."

If I'm not good enough without the Gold Medal, I won't be good enough with it.

What magic. I have or have access to anything I want. Oh My.

Yes I have choices, it's okay to make mistakes. People who aren't doing much don't make many mistakes. What say you?

You don't always get what you want, but if you try you might just get what you need. Bob Dylan.

The highest form of Wisdom is Kindness. The Talmud.

Nodding the head doesn't row the boat. Irish proverb.

One of the most beautiful experiences is the Mysterious. Albert Einstein.

The very pursuit of happiness, thwarts happiness. Victor Frankl.

There's more to life than being happy. Happiness for me is a by-product and ensues.

Everything can be taken from a person but there right to perspective. The freedom to opt for your music, your drummer, your life, your Navajo Peace is priceless in my experience.

I'm picking up good vibrations. Sometimes it's best for me to lower vibrations.

Nice freedom not to be a threat to me or you. I'm a safe person, this wasn't always true in my mental illness.

What is life expecting from me. It's good to have hopes and expectations, yet for me, "It's what is life expecting from me?" Victor Frankl

Tears have both bitter and sweet chemicals. Both are healing.

Friendship may well be reckoned the masterpiece of Nature. Emerson.

I am responsible for the well being of others and myself. I'm responsible to Civilization. Takes a village.

Criticism is always a severe loss of control.

What I resist persists. Carl Jung

They who are not busy being born, are busy dying. —Bob Dylan.

Life is hard, not just to love but to grasp. Bob Dylan.

The Ambiguity of Reality of the answer is blowing in the wind.

Freedom is not having to look for the next high.

Hello darkness my old friend.

Non-Negativity is balance. Martin Seligman.

Four word Ice breaker. Tell me about yourself?

There's Power in healthy boundaries.

There's Power in Win-Win or No Deal.

Leave a little of the Game of Life to God.

How long? Not long! Martin Luther King Jr.

They abolished slavery in 1865.

Failure is a option.

Success in 99% failure. Honda.

Arrogance swims upstream and ultimately dies of exhaustion. Humility and gratitude flows with the river of life into multiple safe secure coves and inlets and recycles and recirculates the rough waves. Bill Hale.

Non-Negative is enough.

Can I detox from toxic drama?

Am I closed minded blindly certain sometimes?

The obvious realities are hard to talk about.

I was a oak, now I'm a willow I can bend.

Can I stop trying to get back to the past?

Am I a safe person? Are there safe spaces?

Can I bargain with Chaos?

Do I have any Secure Bases right now?

King & Pawn go back in the same box.

All sunshine makes the desert.

What on your heart?

Isn't there enough drama with fake news?

———•———

Good to be under the influence and not drunk.

Degrees of honesty practical vs rigorous.

I stay away from the Royal we. Holier thou.

I used to be different, now I'm the same in general

The way out is through usually take a village.

———•———

I like degrees of tolerance, unselfishness.

I've heard we all have stardust in our cells.

Let Stardust settle, it can't when I stir up.
Infinite patience brings immediate patience.

Stop looking to past for explanations.

Is civilization progressing per capita?

———•———

Power is letting the game come to me.

Losers can be winners, winners losers.

Cherish the little things, one day big.

If want to much likely disappointed.

Enron had a investor M.Yass.

Some believe Wall St will correct itself.

The Emperor has no clothes.

Power and fun can go together.

Youd Cassius has a lean and hungry look.

Great power in humor. Why the long face?

One beggar showing another how to find food

I can't change what I don't acknowledge.

Lady had Bumper stick, Custer had it coming.

Intimate dialogue is I/Your=Us.
Monologue is I-it, my way or highway.

I have more problems being right that wrong.

Conclusions, Part II

Full Meaning of Love Neighbor AS yourself?

What hateful to yourself don't do to others!

I know this work has repetitions, hopefully like me the second time or third time you hear they may resonate, sometimes it takes many times before I absorb. Like the word Temporary. Why should I worry about things that are temporary? But I do and burn up energy pining about matter I can't influence. There is lots of grace in know life is very temporary and my daily bread is enough.

I love the idea of Tender Mercies and hope you will take some of these with you.

Yes I like dialogue, but sometimes talking and can make things worse for me. I try to have a cup of shut the blessed up.

Happiness is like a butterfly, the more I chase it the more elusive. When I turn my attention to other matters, sometimes they come and land softly on my shoulders.

Noble silence is powerful for me.

Power is having some skin in the game.

Death is life's way of saying slow down. Slow is real.

Opposite of love isn't hate it's indifference.

It's okay to broom the past.

Doing right doesn't always feel good.

It's China town Jake.

If I can't explain it simply, I don't understand it. Albert Einstein.

Good for me not to talk unless I can improve the silence.

The grateful person knows life is good not from hearsay but from experiences. Thomas Merton.

I'm not crazy about life but it's the only place to get a good meal and sometimes have instant vacations of laughter.

I'm not alone, and I would not intrude the past on my guest. I have invited them and they are here. I need do nothing except not to interfere. A Course in Miracles-Chapter 16.

Hell must be empty, all the devils are here.

Eternity's Sunrise.
Those who bind themselves to a joy, does the winged life destroy. But those who kisses the joy as it flies, lives in Eternity's Sunrise. Wm. Blake.

The power of humility is know my shoulders aren't built to carry the world on them. If I want to save the world I make my bed each morning.

Like footprints in the sand I have been carried more often than not by Civilizations Tender Mercies.

Problems don't age well, solutions do.

Heartfelt appreciation for joining me in this experience.

Power for me is knowing many things I worry about are temporary. The weather, health issues. Rough remark doctors make in ER, All Bleeding stops. Yet not everything is temporary. Dust to dust was not spoken of the Spirit or Soul.

The Infinite is not temporary, eternity is not temporary. A circle has no beginning or end is not temporary. Point I spend a lot of energy resisting what is temporary.

If I don't do some things I'm not good at I will never get better. Okay the paradox is I don't always have to be getting better or be under construction or a work in progress and carry life like a ball and chain.

Maybe I'm better off not poking the bear. Bears are generally not violent, unless I insist on poking. Another best not poke the dragon.

This book has not tried to be a answer to anyone distress, that's for professionals not us amateurs.

Power is like a Attitude Indicator on a airplane panel. It shows my my wings relative to the horizon. If in fog or at night I may feel I'm level yet be spiraling down, like JFK Jr did because he trusted his gut instead of the instruments. Yes again feeling are never wrong, but often highly inaccurate.

I wish you and yours discernment as to your Sources of Power and a light younger heart.

I have enjoyed beyond measure writing this book, my 10th

Bibliography

What If You Were Your Own Best Friend? Kevin Audley.

Captains and Kings. Taylor Caldwell.

Power of Now. Eckhart Tolle.

The Power of Humility —Charles Whitfield.

Power vs. Force. David Hawkins.

Surprised by Joy. C.S. Lewis.

Better Angels of our Nature. Steven Pinker.

The Prophet by Kahlil Gibran

Hazards of Twelve Step Programs and Religious Fanaticism. L. Michael Audley

1. Chasing False Highs and Running from Lows,

2. Can I Bargain with Chaos and Addictions?

L. Michael Audley.

Quiet. Susan Cain.

Stillness Speaks. Eckhart Tolle.

What the Hell is Water. David Wallace Foster.